I See Colors

Colors

by Susan Chen

HOUGHTON MIFFLIN BOSTON • MORRIS PLAINS, NJ

California • Colorado • Georgia • Illinois • New Jersey • Texas

I have a balloon.
It is red.

I have a flower.
It is yellow.

I have a sweater.
It is green.

I have a teddy bear.
It is brown.

I have a crayon.
It is purple.

I have a pumpkin.
It is orange.

I have a ball.
It is blue.